Management Training for School Leaders: The Academy Concept

by
Arlene H. Patterson

Library of Congress Catalog Number 83-61785
ISBN 0-87367-198-8
Copyright © 1983 by Phi Delta Kappa Educational Foundation
Bloomington, Indiana

This fastback is sponsored by the Homewood Illinois Chapter of Phi Delta Kappa, which made a generous contribution toward publication costs.

The chapter sponsors this fastback to celebrate the 20th anniversary of its founding on November 29, 1962.

Table of Contents

Introduction

School leaders are America's most important executives. With a budget in the billions of dollars and a clientele of more than 46 million students, they manage the single most important enterprise in our nation. However, until recently, the professional competence of the administrators who manage this huge enterprise was largely taken for granted. School leaders received little opportunity and even less incentive to acquire basic management skills that, in the private sector, have marked the difference between success and failure.

Front line managers — principals and superintendents — are often expected to perform as fully developed chief executive officers even though they may have little preparation in the basic management skills considered essential in any effective organization — including schools and school districts.

A survey conducted by the National Center for Education Statistics indicated school administrators perceive a need for improved or expanded training to perform their jobs effectively. Those surveyed rated as "urgent" the need for improved training in community and taxpayer support, energy management, budget management and finance, program evaluation, staff evaluation, implementing state and federal programs, and curriclum development. Those surveyed also said their jobs require training in public relations and media usage, school board relations and governance, issues involving teacher and noncertified personnel unions, implementing civil rights compliance, and organizational structure and development. Although this study concerned superintendents, the authors consider it highly applicable to other staff personnel, especially principals. The authors of this study conclude: "There is a widespread need for expanded training activities in a wide spectrum of administrative responsibilities."

Education agencies and organizations, including colleges of education, acknowledge that management development is important for school administrators. Thousands of educators are engaged in management development, especially in the areas of budget and finance, legal analysis, computer literacy, time and stress management, and negotiating skills. But the situation today is compounded because the school administrator, caught in an economic paradox of simultaneous inflation and recession, must respond to a public that wants to cut taxes and governmental services, and at the same time respond to demands from school employees for higher salaries and increased benefits. If public school administrators are to function successfully in this current situation, they must master the art of management.

Leaders who functioned effectively in the past are finding that they are often not equipped to assume the role thrust on them by the times and the demanding clientele they serve. Efforts to address the problem are increasing as more national, state, and local education agencies respond to the needs of their executive educators. Outstanding among these efforts are the "academies" that are funded, supported, and sometimes staffed by state education agencies. Although the academies differ in agenda, curriculum, and financing, each has as its goal the improvement of the management skills of school administrators. Each academy adheres to the fundamentals outlined by Luvern Cunningham in "An Academy for Personal and Professional Development: Dimensions of a Model" (*California Journal of Teacher Education*, 1981). Each academy provides simultaneously for individual human needs and organizational requirements. And each academy uses a delivery system of proven operational components.

The Academy Concept

The Academy concept, as used in this context, describes an association of programs and events through which training or instruction is made available to school leaders under the auspices of a state education agency. Staffing and funding are the responsibility of the state agency, and the clientele are the administrators served by that agency. Such academies, patterned after similar "institutes" and "universities" offered by private-sector organizations (e.g., General Motors Institute, Disney University, and Holiday Inn University), have evolved into a management and leadership concept unique to education.

Once a state education agency undertakes a commitment to provide an academy training program (often after legislative initiative has earmarked adequate funding for a long-term project), several issues immediately arise:

1. Who will be trained?
2. Who will do the training?
3. What skills will be taught?
4. When and where will training occur?

By asking these questions, several assumptions have already been made concerning the state's appropriate role in providing management training for its school leaders. Among these are the following:

1. There is a body of management knowledge and skills that school leaders should acquire.
2. Such knowledge and skills make a positive difference in the performance of school leaders.

3. Such knowledge and skills can be presented through an academy program offered by the state education agency.
4. School leaders will be motivated to attend academy programs and will benefit from this training.

Who Will Be Trained?

Principals are the primary target audience for academy training programs and, indeed, North Carolina includes principals in its academy's name. However, most academy programs are available to a larger audience — identified as "school leaders" or "school executives." The most wide-ranging programs include assistant principals, principals, supervisors, central office staff, and superintendents and may also extend to those individuals identified (sometimes through assessment center evaluations) as having potential for these leadership positions. Florida extends participation to interested school board members, department of education officials and staff, and leaders of state education agencies.

Who Will Do the Training?

The first management academies tended to follow a safe course by utilizing trainers with recognized expertise. Generally this meant employing staff from the two most successful and prestigious training groups: the American Management Association — the leading trainer for the nation's corporate leaders — and the National Academy for School Executives — the training arm of the American Association of School Administrators. Later, as the academy concept gained acceptance, the tendency has been to turn training over entirely or partly to "local experts" available through the state department of education, school districts, colleges and universities, or business and industry. To meet specific local needs, academies often develop in-house trainers who have firsthand knowledge in specialty areas such as collective bargaining and school finance. Experienced outside consultants are used when their expertise is essential to the topic.

What Skills Should Be Taught?

The academy's curriculum is usually determined by conducting a needs assessment among all levels of management, assistant principals through superintendents; although, especially where principals are the target audience (as in North Carolina and Maryland), the assessment may be limited to principals.

When and Where Shall Training Occur?

Training may occur at a location within the state department of education facility, a special state-owned training facility, in school district facilities, or in traditional commercial conference centers in local hotels and motels. Often training seminars, institutes, or programs are repeated at several locations within each state to make these programs more accessible to school leaders statewide.

The length of these seminars varies from state to state. Some hold special one-day sessions for specific one-time purposes. For example, Florida holds a one-day "Legislative Update" once each year. Maryland finds its greatest success with five-day residential retreats at either of two permanent locations. Pennsylvania offers similar retreats lasting two or three days. Most academies sponsor two-day sessions. For example, Florida, North Carolina, and South Carolina each hold two-day "School Law" seminars.

Several academies also offer programs to coincide with other statewide meetings. For example, North Carolina offers a "Stress Management" institute at the same location and time that the North Carolina Principals Association holds it annual convention. Florida plans a session each year to coincide with the annual conference of the state's superintendents association.

The Academies

Academy programs began in the late 1970s at the state level when Pennsylvania included school leaders in its overall school improvement process. At about the same time at the national level, several top executive officers from the public sector, including several chief state school officers, were exposed to management development through involvement in a series of programs offered through the American Management Association (AMA) and the National Academy for School Executives (NASE). Today there are an increasing number of academy programs offered by education agencies. The five described below are perhaps the most sophisticated and thus might serve as models for other states.

North Carolina Leadership Institute for Principals

The North Carolina Leadership Institute for Principals (NCLIP) is a program of the North Carolina Department of Public Instruction and is headed by a special assistant to the superintendent. In 1979 the North Carolina legislature allocated $500,000 for the biennium, supplemented by federal monies.

NCLIP offers a series of three- to five-day staff development seminars for the state's 2,000 principals. Seminars are conducted in each region of the state to minimize travel for participants. Training topics include teacher evaluation, discipline alternatives, school law, principles of management, and time and stress management. Presenters (trainers) are selected from practitioners and theoreticians; sometimes these are North Carolina educators, but outside consultants are also used. All expenses for participants are paid by the state education agency.

Internships. Short internship programs are available through NCLIP. Selected school leaders are matched with other individuals (or assigned to other programs) to address their specific, assessed needs. Typically, a principal who perceives a weakness in a skill interns briefly with either another principal or a business leader who has outstanding skills in that area. Also long-term internships are available each year to three principals within the state; those selected are granted a one-year leave of absence from a cooperating school district. The interns function as full-time members of the institute staff. Their job responsibilities range from managing special projects to presenting seminars.

Human Resource Bank. A human resource data bank identifies outstanding individuals who can serve as a resource for school districts planning staff development in management skills. The data bank also links districts with outstanding programs.

Computer Training. A microcomputer demonstration center is housed at the institute. Software packets developed by institute staff are available to assist with scheduling, keeping track of student attendance, inventory, and other record-keeping tasks. Computers, training programs, and software packages are available for use by principals.

Florida Academy for School Leaders

The Florida Academy for School Leaders (FASL) was created by the Florida legislature in 1978 through its Management Training Act, the only legislation in the nation that prescribes a comprehensive plan to improve the management skills of school leaders. FASL, which began operating in 1980, supplements the traditional preparation programs offered by colleges and universities. There is no charge to attend the FASL institutes. Travel and lodging for participants are paid by school districts from their staff development funds.

Unlike programs in other states, Florida's management training program is the responsibility of a Council on Educational Management appointed by the governor. The members of this council include executive officers from public agencies, including a deputy commissioner of education; a school superintendent; several principals; and executives from Florida corporations such as the Tampa Electric Company. The council is mandated to:

1. Identify competencies that characterize high-performing principals.
2. Identify standards and procedures for measuring and evaluating performance of those competencies.
3. Identify the training process required for principals and other managers to acquire those competencies.
4. Develop training materials not otherwise available.
5. Identify procedures necessary to implement a program of competency certification for school managers.
6. Develop policies and procedures necessary to implement a compensation program for principals and other managers that is based on successful performance of the identified competencies.
7. Identify criteria for screening, selecting, and appointing principals and other managers.

FASL is mandated to provide inservice training for school managers at all levels of the public school system. In 1981, $600,000 was provided for operation of the Florida academy.

FASL serves 67 Florida school districts through a series of 14 different programs offered several times each year in 10 regional locations. Prior to 1982, programs were provided through a contractual arrangement with the National Academy for School Executives, as well as through in-house Florida Department of Education programs. Beginning in 1982, however, such contractual agreements with groups outside the state are no longer permitted. Academy programs are developed instate through cooperative efforts with Florida colleges and universities and other education organizations and agencies.

Grant Programs. School districts compete for grants by submitting proposals for programs designed to train district administrators, principals, and potential candidates for such positions. Some funds are paid by the district, with the state providing the remainder through management grants. Technical assistance is also provided by the academy or through special contractual arrangements with universities. Other funding for management development programs is available through the state

school-based Management Project Grants and through a special category of Title IV-C federal grants.

Maryland Professional Development Academy

The Maryland Professional Development Academy (MPDA) has grown from four state regional institutes offered for the first time in 1978 to eight statewide institutes with more than 200 participants in 1981. The Maryland academy is part of the Bureau of Staff Development in the Maryland State Department of Education and therefore receives no special budget allocations.

MPDA program offerings concentrate on curriculum areas rather than "pure" management skills. Topics include "The OK Administrator," "Moving from Segregation to Integration," and "Increasing Teacher Effectiveness." A series of 10 five-day programs, each serving 30 participants, are held at two retreat locations. The goal of each program is the development of a project to be implemented by individual participants when they return to their district. About three months after the program, a follow-up session is arranged to enable participants to share their progress with each other and their instructor and to refine their project. A second follow-up session is held several months later. Finally, a one-day evaluation/recommendation session is held to assess the success of the project and possible further refinement for implementation. Academy staff view evaluation of the projects and of the overall program as critical components of the training process in order to improve future MPDA programs.

MPDA's development has been part of a statewide emphasis on staff development programs offered by all education agencies. The Maryland Council of Staff Developers was formed in the late 1970s to help ensure inservice coordination among agencies and districts and to offer assistance in defining the nature and direction of all state programs. The council has encouraged programs that are comprehensive and directly linked to local efforts.

Pennsylvania Executive Academy

The Pennsylvania Executive Academy is one component in Pennsylvania's comprehensive training network for school improvement.

Other components include an inservice network, school improvement orientations and administrative planning, educational quality assessment, school equity desegregation assistance, management assistance teams, and an officers leadership institute. The academy offers programs for teachers and administrators from local school districts, intermediate units, and institutions of higher education. Programs focus on aspects of problem solving, management skills, and special interests.

The Academy was formed in the early 1970s and is part of the Bureau of School Improvement. The academy provides 35 to 40 seminars each year to 1,000 executive-level personnel. Participants may enroll as individuals or as administrative teams. Seminars last from one to four days depending on the topic. Topics include forecasting outcomes, instructional leadership, global education, conflict management, and delegation of authority. Expenses for travel and lodging are paid either by the participant or by the local school district.

South Carolina Administrators Leadership Academy

The South Carolina Administrators Leadership Academy (SCALA), which began operation in July 1981, is a cooperative venture of the State Department of Education, the University of South Carolina, and Sumter School District. It is administered by the department of education through the Office of Accreditation and Administrative Services. The University of South Carolina and Sumter School District provide support services. Through collaborative efforts with school districts, higher education, education consortia, and professional associations, SCALA offers administrative training programs in management skill development, seminars on current issues, and programs on problem solving.

SCALA's management skill development programs include seminars on office management, time and stress management, personnel evaluation, program design, group dynamics, and effective communication. The seminars on current issues focus on coping with job-related problems, legislative changes, and strategic planning. The programs on problem solving are designed to help school districts identify and analyze problems, find alternative solutions, and develop strategies for enacting change.

At this writing other academy management development programs are operating through the state education department in Alabama and through universities at Auburn University in Montgomery and the University of Oregon. Several local school districts (e.g., Memphis City Schools; Dade County, Florida; and Greenville, South Carolina) have excellent programs in management training for their school leaders. Currently, eight states (Alabama, Colorado, Florida, Georgia, Maryland, North Carolina, Pennsylvania, and South Carolina) have management training programs at the state level and 12 states have programs available through public education agencies.

Variations on a Theme:
The Business/Industry Liaison

The North Carolina Department of Public Instruction, through its Leadership Institute for Principals (NCLIP), was the first academy program in the nation to establish a Business Liaison Program, a partnership with local business and industry in management development. Business and industry provide sophisticated management training programs for their employees that are generic enough to have value for managers and leaders in education. NCLIP has identified several North Carolina corporations that offer such programs and are willing to accept principals as participants. The institute serves as liaison between principal and program and helps defray the cost of the training (if applicable) and pays for travel expenses.

The private sector can offer human resources and services and can tailor its programs to the leadership needs of its administrators. The participating North Carolina corporations provide a community service and expand the influence of their training and development programs, while the Business Liaison Program increases the opportunities for management development for educators beyond what is available through programs offered by state and local education agencies. Since its inception in early 1982, the program has flourished and now includes management training by Burlington Industries, Carolina Light and Power Company, CIBA-GEIGY, IBM, and P. Lorillard.

The Memphis City School Academy has begun an exchange program with local business and industry. Private sector executives offer the same professional services that they perform for their employers in their company training programs. Executives from the Federal Express Company and Holiday Inns, Inc. recently assisted the Memphis superintendent in conducting a series of studies that included an assessment of the training needs of top management in the school system.

In Florida, the Council of 100 (representing 100 of that state's top corporations) is looking for specific ways to provide cooperative programs with education agencies. One program being considered is a mutual exchange, with school administrators participating in programs offered by local business, and local business participating in programs offered by the Florida Academy for School Leaders.

Another example of school/business cooperation in management training was a national symposium held in Florida in 1981. Executives from General Motors Institute, Disney University, Tampa Electric Company, American Management Association, and the Milton Roy Corporation met with the directors of the five state management training academies; chief school officers from Florida, Maryland, Georgia, Pennsylvania, Mississippi, and North Carolina; and executives from the major national education organizations, including Phi Delta Kappa. The symposium was the first in a series of national conferences to explore the role of state education agencies in providing management training for school executives. A key ingredient in the symposium was the private sector viewpoint.

Conclusion

Florida is one of a growing number of states whose leaders openly support state funding for management training for school leaders. Bob Graham, governor of Florida and president of the Education Commission of the States, believes such training is needed to provide schools with the leadership that quality education demands:

> It is well known that effective and efficient management of schools requires a blend of skills, experience, and academic background rarely provided through baccalaureate or graduate programs in education.

Ralph Turlington, commissioner of education for the state of Florida, reinforces Governor Graham's views when he states:

> To be an educational leader in the Eighties is to have experienced frustration with the inadequate education available in traditional pre-service programs, for it is no longer reasonable to expect our colleges and universities to do the job alone. Today's educational leader must also be an educational manager. Today's manager must be prepared to respond to changes in state and federal mandate, to manage resources, to work miracles with a shrinking budget, and analyze and synthesize an incredible amount of data — all in an effort to improve the quality of education services related to increased student achievement.

Ernest Boyer, former U.S. commissioner of education, and Milton Goldberg, former acting director of the National Institute of Education, cite poor management as a major factor in the decline in public education. They point to research that shows an effective principal is one with good management skills. They suggest that if the key word for education in the Eighties is excellence, then we can expect nothing less from those who manage the business of education.

Most school leaders define their success in terms of student achievement; i.e., a good school or school district is one in which students achieve. Research supports that conclusion, so does the public perception and common sense; but school leaders are finding this equation to be simplistic. For example, although school principals describe their role as that of curriculum leader, those same principals often report their daily time consumption in terms of management activities, not curriculum tasks.

As school leaders struggle with declining enrollment, increasing costs, judicial and legislative intervention, and collective bargaining, they conclude over and over again that successful performance on the job requires them to be more than curriculum leaders. To be an educational leader means having the skills to manage schools and school districts effectively so that students may achieve.

Does participation in a management academy make a difference in the effectiveness of school leaders? Yes, according to a 1982 survey of academy participants in Florida, Maryland, and North Carolina. These school leaders said they benefited personally and professionally; and they credit the academy for their ability to become more efficient, productive, and generally happier educational leaders.

A sampling of responses from participants in the survey captures their feelings:

So many times principals came from the classroom into their jobs without much to go on in the way of helping teachers to be better. Courses in administration on the college level oftentimes do not prepare principals for this. . . . It is becoming crucial that administrators have some training experiences to keep staff members from becoming stagnant. Management training gives school leaders more confidence in training teachers and dealing with school problems.

* * *

They have been the most rewarding experiences professionally that I've had. The presenters have been excellent, and I've been able to use much of the content in my job. I believe I am more competent in my job, and per-

21

sonal relationships have improved. . . . The entire program was first class.

* * *

I came away extremely fired up to do something with all the information I received. The sessions rejuvenated my spirit.

* * *

It is an accepted fact that good management is necessary for a school program to operate smoothly. Education is big business and good management is required. Teachers respond to management or lack thereof.

* * *

Management training makes a difference in the way individuals administer their schools.

* * *

School leaders tend to be isolated in their jobs. . . . They benefit a great deal from coming together to share concerns and innovative solutions to problems.

* * *

I expect more from my teachers now and they in turn expect more from their students. More important, I am able to suggest ideas for improved teaching techniques that have made a difference.

* * *

These programs are the best thing that has happened to education in many years.

* * *

If principals manage better, schools run smoother, use resources more effectively; these benefit students in the long run.

The educational leader of the Eighties must be financial manager, skillful negotiator, manager of human resources, and source of legal knowledge. The academy concept is the means to effect this impressive array of abilities.